AF588484

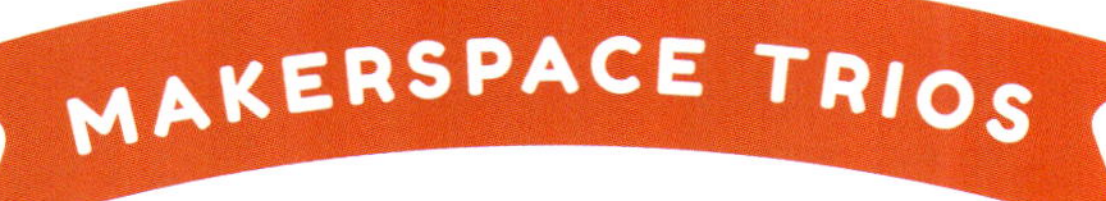


# Creating with EGG CARTONS, STRING & STRAWS

Elsie Olson

Consulting Editor, Diane Craig, M.A./Reading Specialist

Super Sandcastle

An Imprint of Abdo Publishing
abdobooks.com

**abdobooks.com**

Published by Abdo Publishing, a division of ABDO, PO Box 398166, Minneapolis, Minnesota 55439. 

Printed in the United States of America, North Mankato, Minnesota
102021
012022

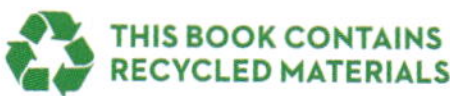
THIS BOOK CONTAINS RECYCLED MATERIALS

Design: Sarah DeYoung, Mighty Media, Inc.
Production: Mighty Media, Inc.
Editor: Megan Borgert-Spaniol
Cover Photographs: iStockphoto; Mighty Media, Inc.; Shutterstock Images
Interior Photographs: 文波/Flickr; iStockphoto; Mighty Media, Inc.; Picasa/Flickr; Shutterstock Images; Tim Hammond/No10 Downing Street/Flickr

The following manufacturers/names appearing in this book are trademarks: Crayola®, Elmer's®, Farmers Hen House

Library of Congress Control Number: 2021943016

**Publisher's Cataloging-in-Publication Data**
Names: Olson, Elsie, author.
Title: Creating with egg cartons, string & straws / by Elsie Olson
Description: Minneapolis, Minnesota : Abdo Publishing, 2022 | Series: Makerspace trios | Includes online resources and index.
Identifiers: ISBN 9781532196423 (lib. bdg.) | ISBN 9781098218232 (ebook)
Subjects: LCSH: Handicraft--Juvenile literature. | Creative thinking--Juvenile literature. | String craft--Juvenile literature. | Egg carton craft--Juvenile literature. | Drinking straws--Juvenile literature. | Mixed media crafts--Juvenile literature.
Classification: DDC 745.5--dc23

Super SandCastle™ books are created by a team of professional educators, reading specialists, and content developers around five essential components—phonemic awareness, phonics, vocabulary, text comprehension, and fluency—to assist young readers as they develop reading skills and strategies and increase their general knowledge. All books are written, reviewed, and leveled for guided reading and early reading intervention programs for use in shared, guided, and independent reading and writing activities to support a balanced approach to literacy instruction.

## TO ADULT HELPERS

The projects in this book are fun and simple. There are just a few things to remember to keep kids safe. Some projects may use sharp or hot objects. Also, kids may be using messy supplies. Make sure they protect their clothes and work surfaces. Be ready to offer guidance during brainstorming and assist when necessary.

# CONTENTS

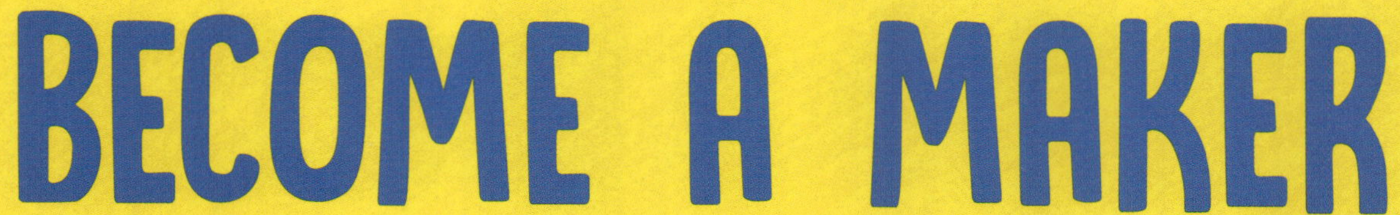

# BECOME A MAKER

A makerspace is like a laboratory. It's a place where ideas are formed and problems are solved. Kids like you create amazing things in makerspaces. Many makerspaces are in schools and libraries. But they can also be in kitchens, bedrooms, and backyards. Anywhere can be a makerspace when you use imagination, inspiration, **collaboration**, and problem-solving!

## Imagination

This takes you to new places and lets you experience new things. Anything is possible with imagination!

## Inspiration

This is the spark that gives you an idea. Inspiration can come from almost anywhere!

# Makerspace Toolbox

## Collaboration

Makers work together. They ask questions and get ideas from everyone around them. Collaboration solves problems that seem impossible.

## Problem-Solving

Things often don't go as planned when you're creating. But that's part of the fun! Find creative solutions to any problem that comes up. These will make your project even better.

# EXPLORE EGG CARTONS

You've probably seen egg cartons before. Maybe you even have some in your refrigerator! Egg cartons can be made of plastic, foam, or recycled bits of cardboard and paper.

## Egg Carton Properties

- Flexible
- Lightweight
- Smooth
- Sturdy

### How Can You Use Egg Cartons?

Egg cartons are usually used to hold chicken eggs. But you can use egg cartons however you like in a makerspace! Let your imagination wander. What would it look like to use egg cartons in a new way?

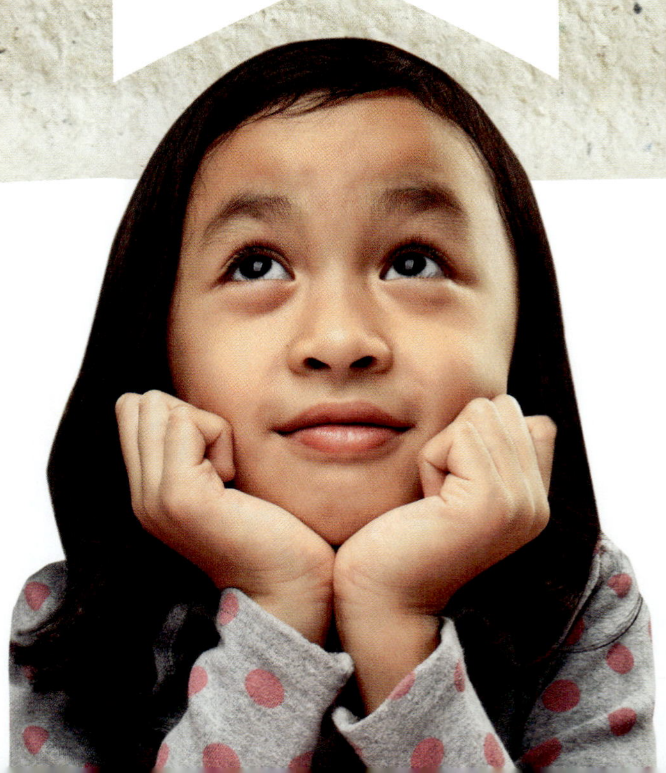

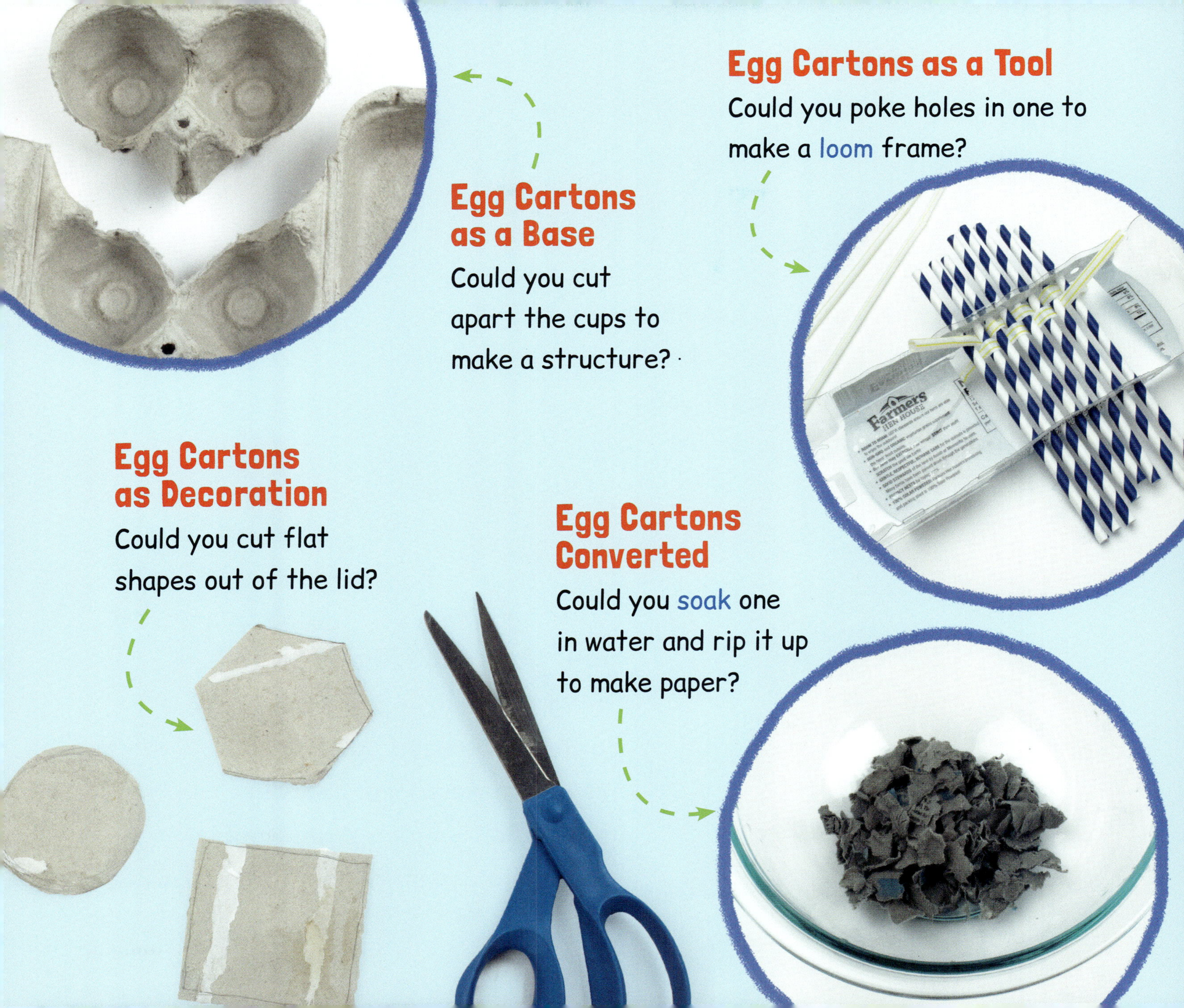


## Egg Cartons as a Tool

Could you poke holes in one to make a loom frame?

## Egg Cartons as a Base

Could you cut apart the cups to make a structure?

## Egg Cartons as Decoration

Could you cut flat shapes out of the lid?

## Egg Cartons Converted

Could you soak one in water and rip it up to make paper?

# EXPLORE STRING

String is made from individual fibers twisted together. It is used for binding, hanging, and more. You might use string to tie your shoes, catch some fish, sew clothes, and more!

## String Properties

- Flexible
- Long
- Strong
- Thin

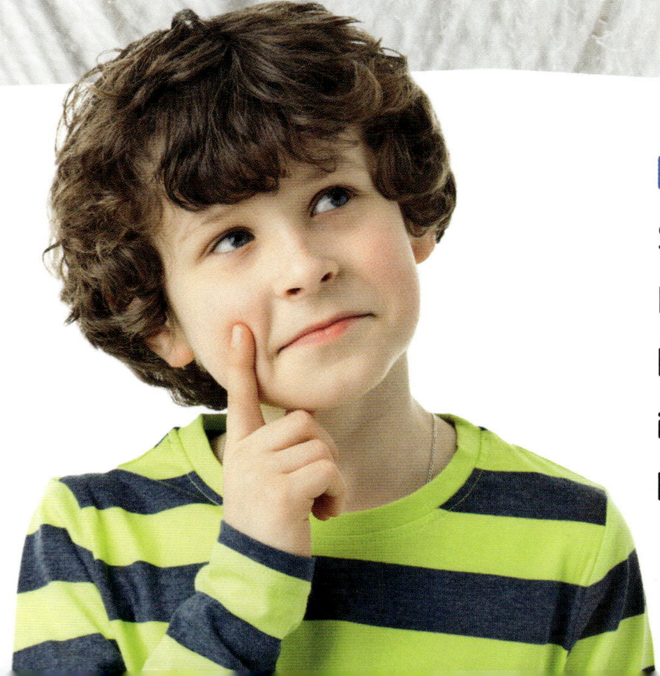

### How Can You Use String?

String has many practical purposes. But it can be used however you like in a makerspace! Let your imagination wander. What would it look like to use string in a new way?

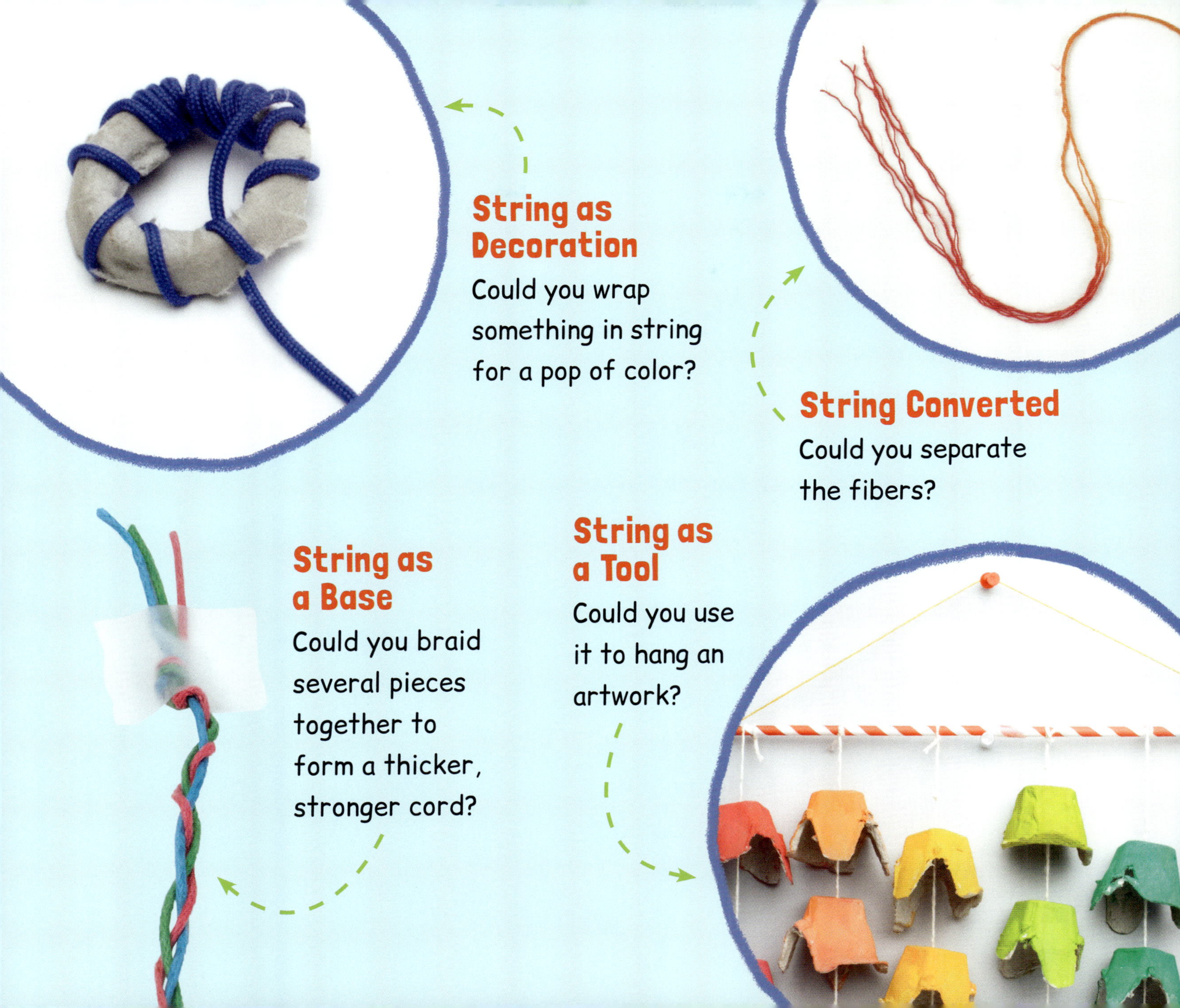

## String as Decoration

Could you wrap something in string for a pop of color?

## String Converted

Could you separate the fibers?

## String as a Base

Could you braid several pieces together to form a thicker, stronger cord?

## String as a Tool

Could you use it to hang an artwork?

# EXPLORE STRAWS

Straws come in handy when you are drinking a tall glass of soda or water. Some straws are straight. Others are curved. They can be made of paper, cardboard, plastic, or even metal!

## Straw Properties

- Flexible
- Hollow
- Lightweight
- Stiff

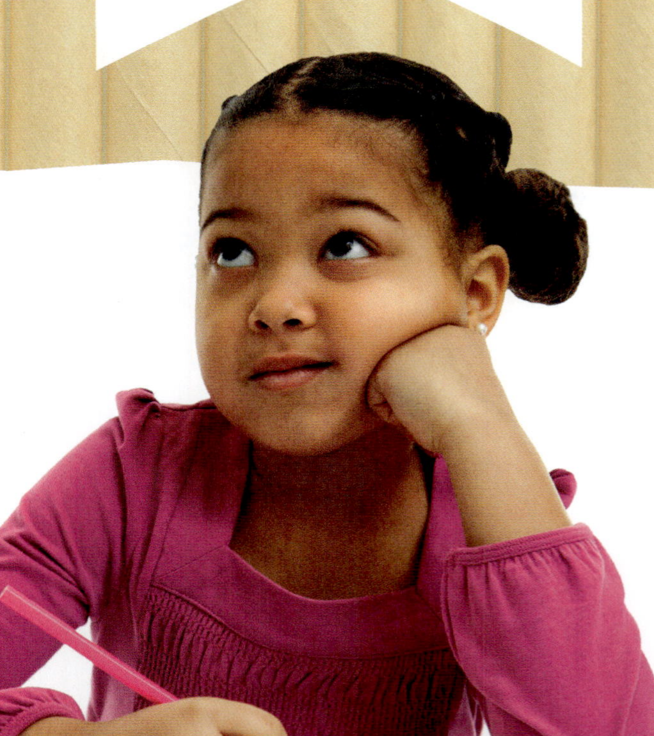

### How Can You Use Straws?

Straws are most often used as a drinking tool. But they can be used however you like in a makerspace! Let your imagination wander. What would it look like to use straws in a new way?

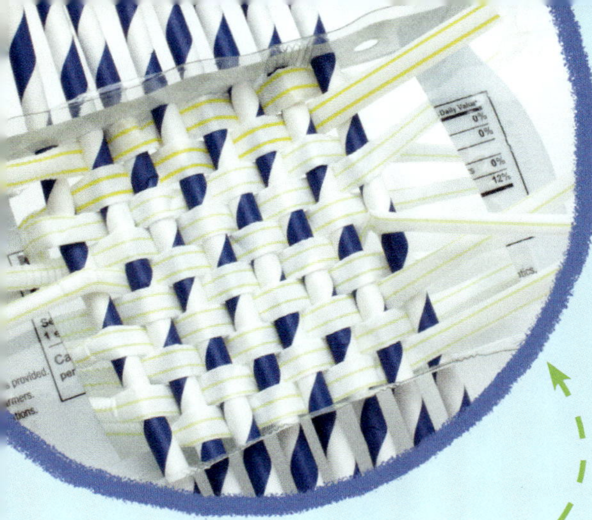

## Straws as Decoration

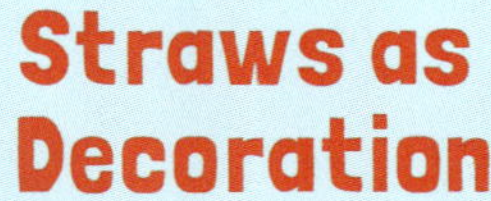

Could you cut them into small pieces to make antennae, eyes, or spikes?

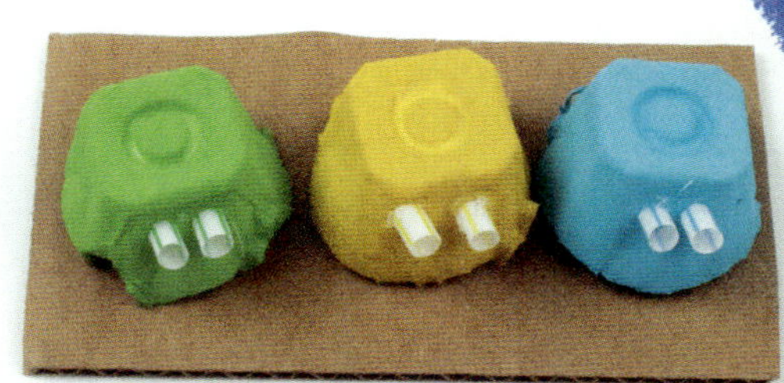

## Straws as a Base

Could you weave them together to make a flat surface?

## Straws Converted

Could you cut them in half or punch holes in them to give them a completely new shape?

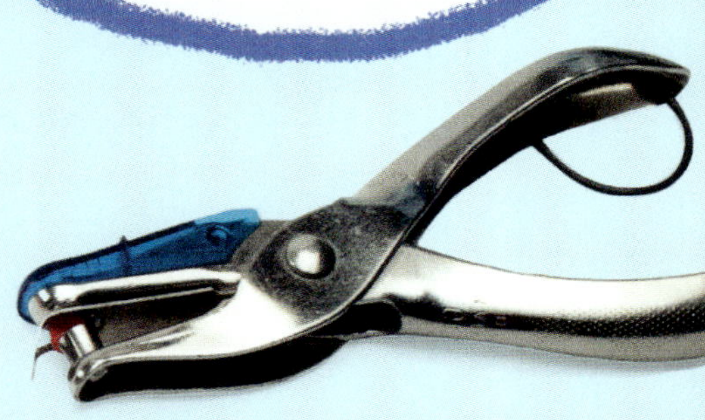

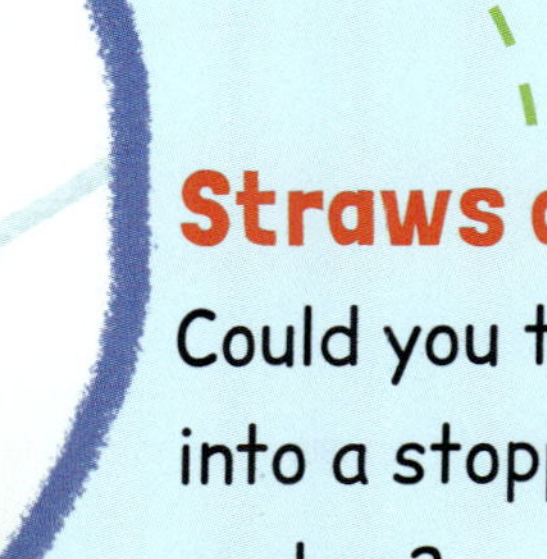

## Straws as a Tool

Could you turn one into a stopper or anchor?

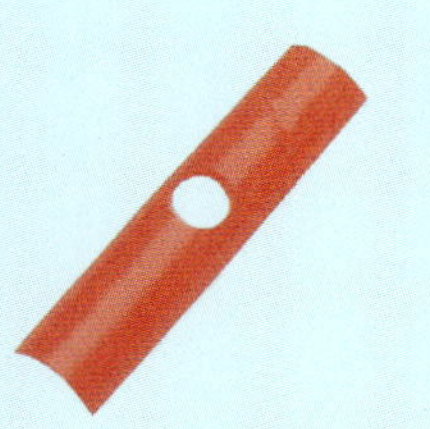

# GET INSPIRED

People have used egg cartons, string, and straws in all kinds of creative ways. Let these examples spark your imagination!

Paper-based egg cartons break down in soil. You can use them to grow seedlings. Then you can plant the entire egg carton in your garden!

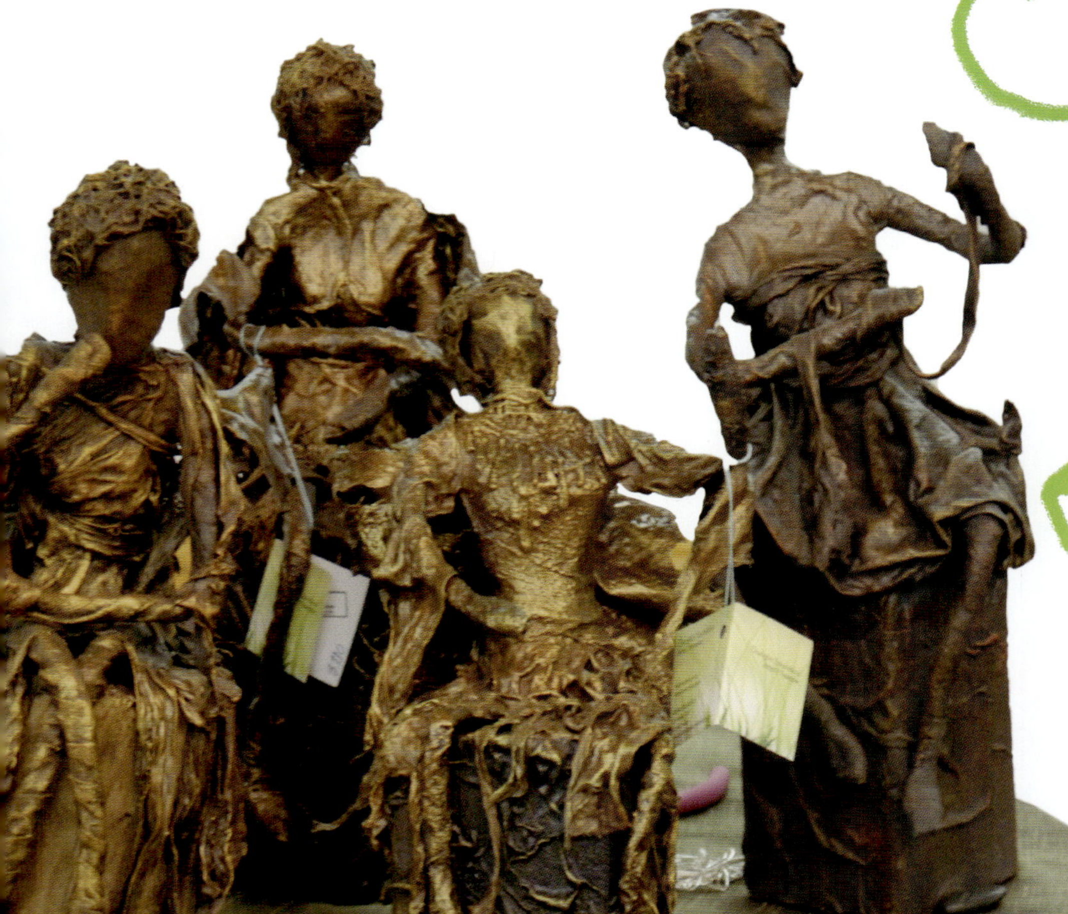

Egg cartons are broken down in boiling water and then shaped into sculptures.

A rainbow string art display in London, England

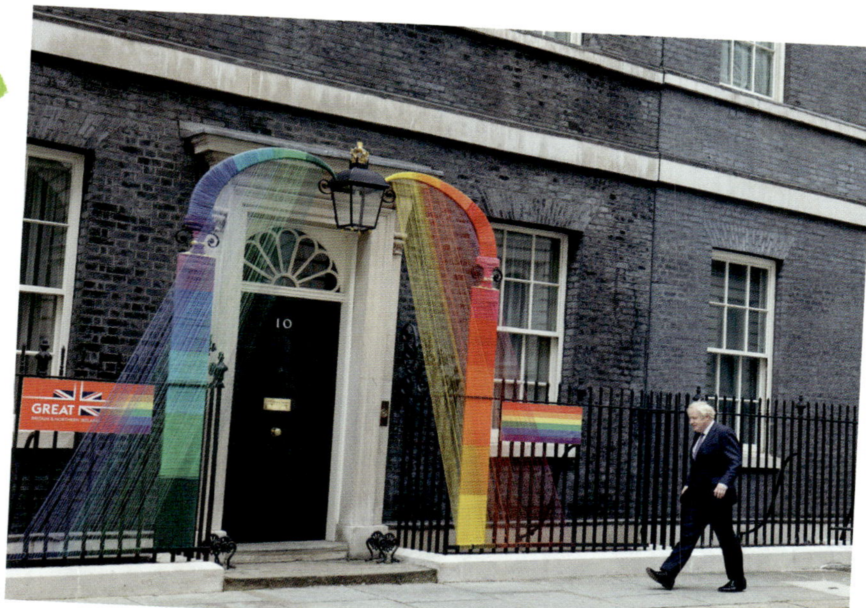


Straw art

Some artists make art by wrapping string around nails.

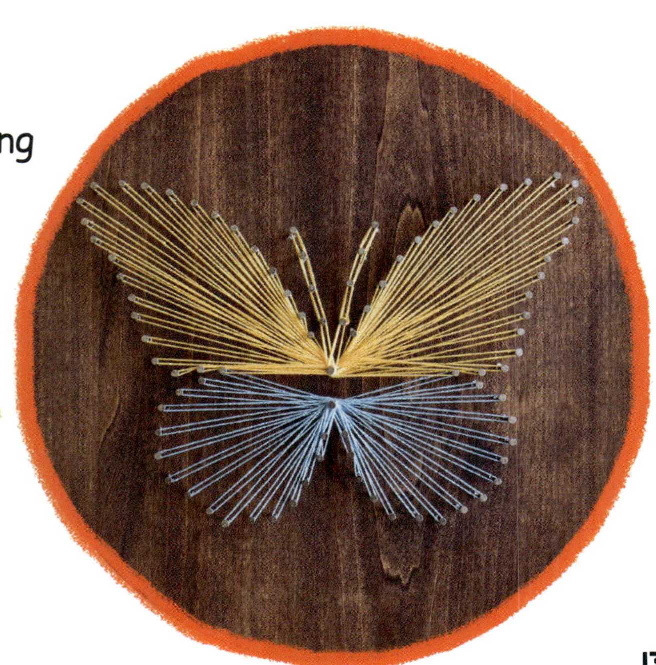

# MAKER TOOLS

Are you inspired? Have you brainstormed some makerspace projects? It's time to gather your egg cartons, string, and straws. You may also need a few everyday tools to cut and connect your primary materials.

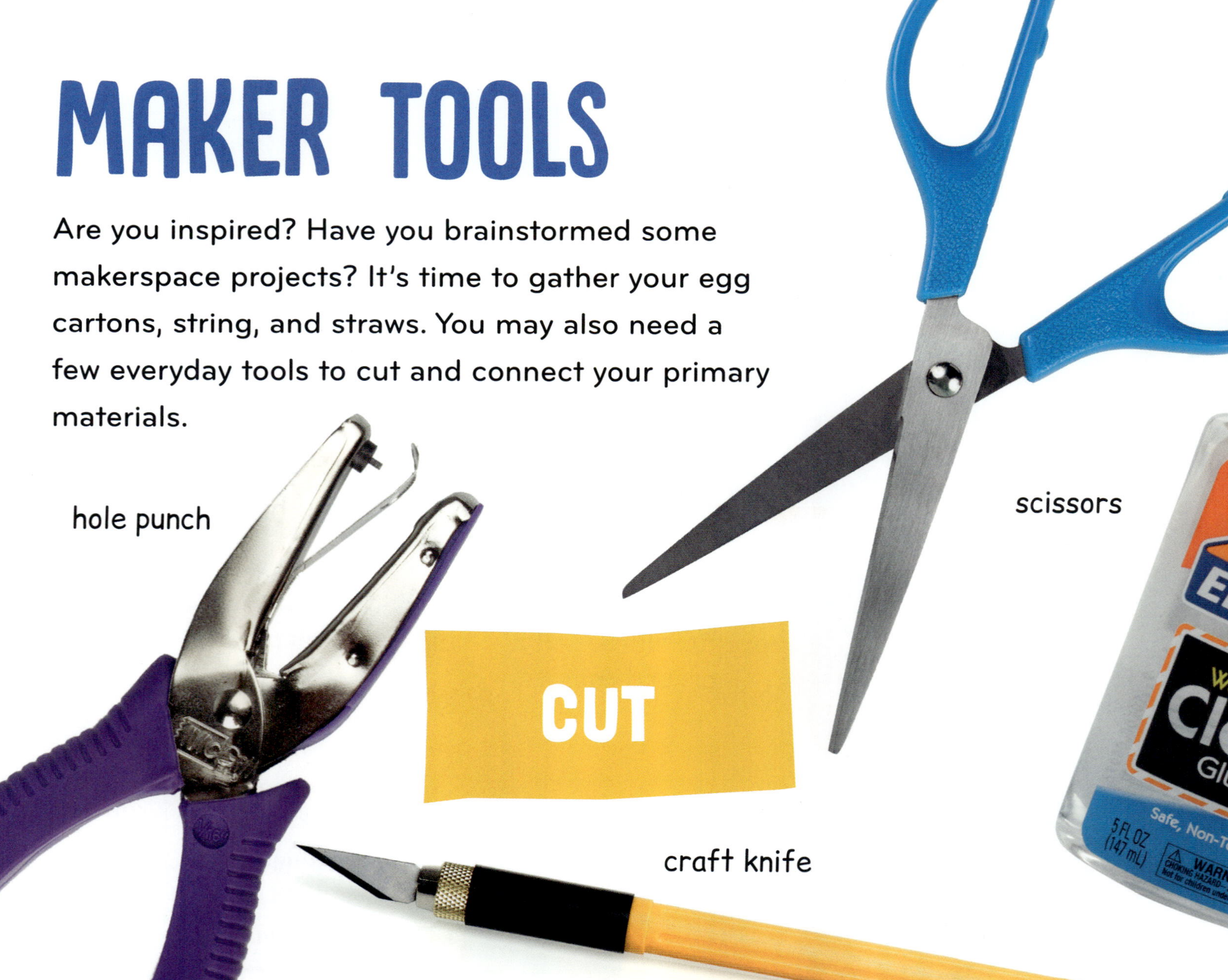

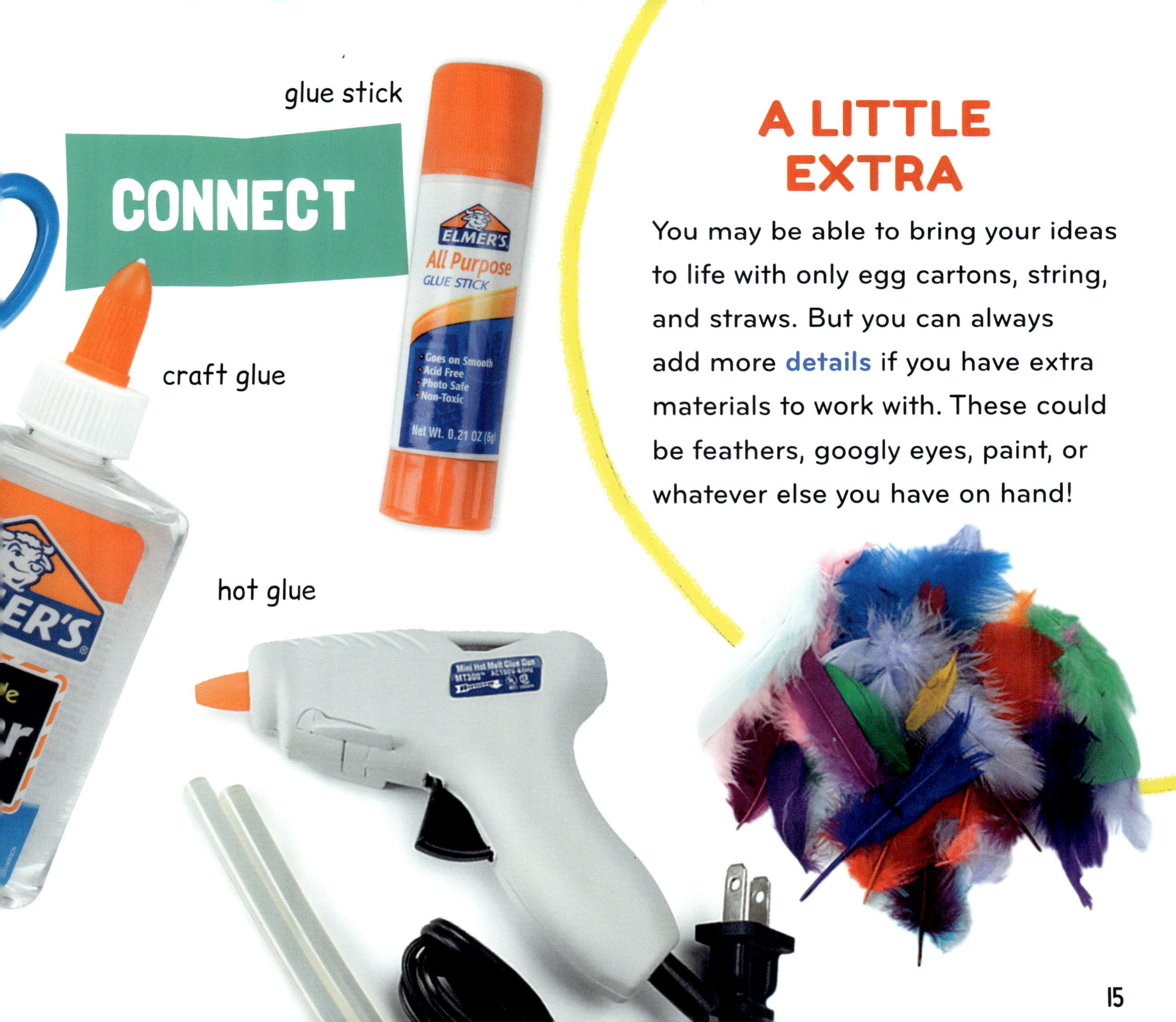


## A LITTLE EXTRA

You may be able to bring your ideas to life with only egg cartons, string, and straws. But you can always add more **details** if you have extra materials to work with. These could be feathers, googly eyes, paint, or whatever else you have on hand!

# MAKING YOUR MAKERSPACE

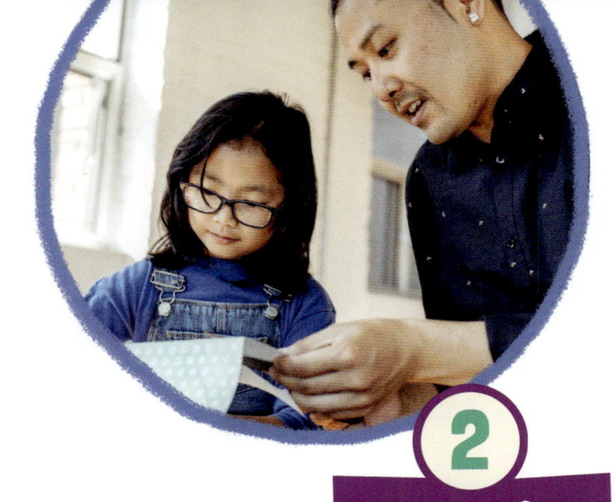

You can let your imagination run wild in a makerspace. But be sure to follow these rules to stay safe and be respectful.

## 1 Gather your materials

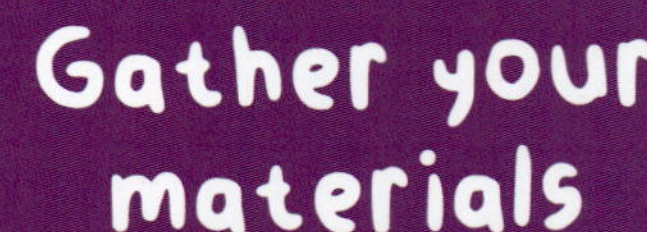

Make sure an adult says it's OK to use what you gather.

## 2 Be safe

Ask an adult for help when using sharp or hot tools, such as craft knives or glue guns.

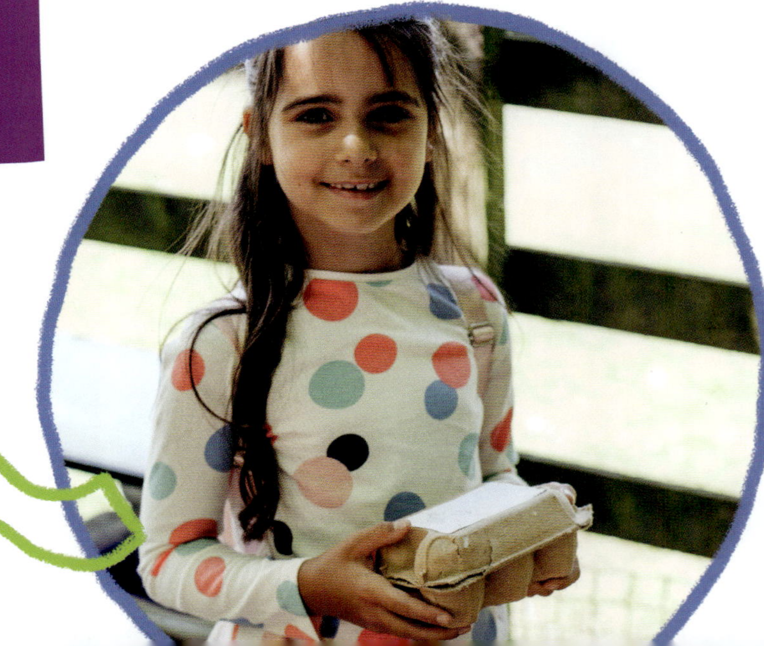

## Share the space

Share supplies and space with other makers. You can invite them to share their ideas if you're feeling stuck!

## Keep trying

Don't give up when things don't go exactly as planned. Instead, think about the problem you are having. What are some ways to solve it?

## Clean up

Put away materials. Find a safe space to store unfinished projects until next time. And clean up any scraps, spills, or messes you made.

# DISPLAY IT

Create hanging artwork from egg cartons, string, and straws. Then put it on display!

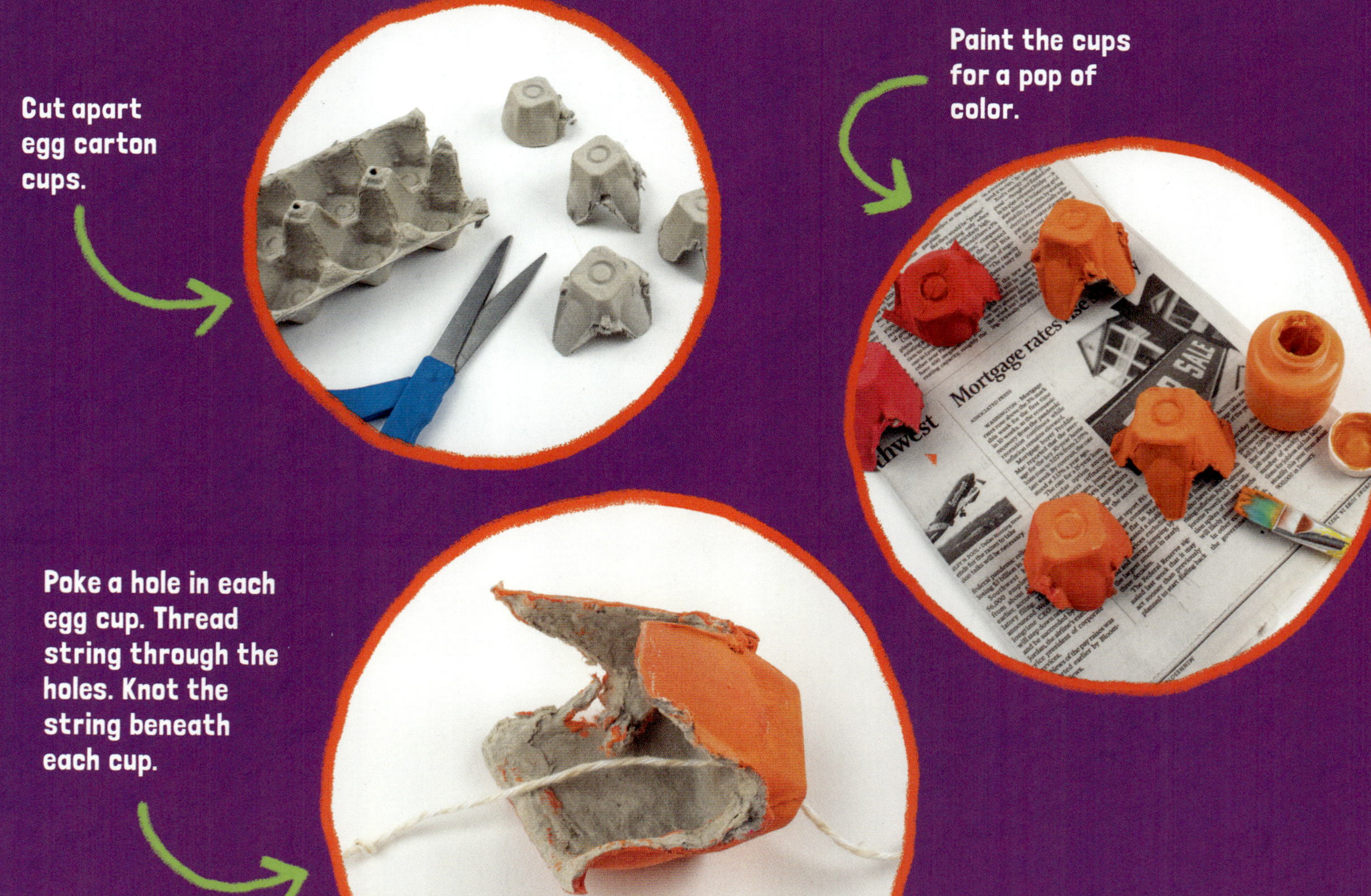


Cut apart egg carton cups.

Paint the cups for a pop of color.

Poke a hole in each egg cup. Thread string through the holes. Knot the string beneath each cup.

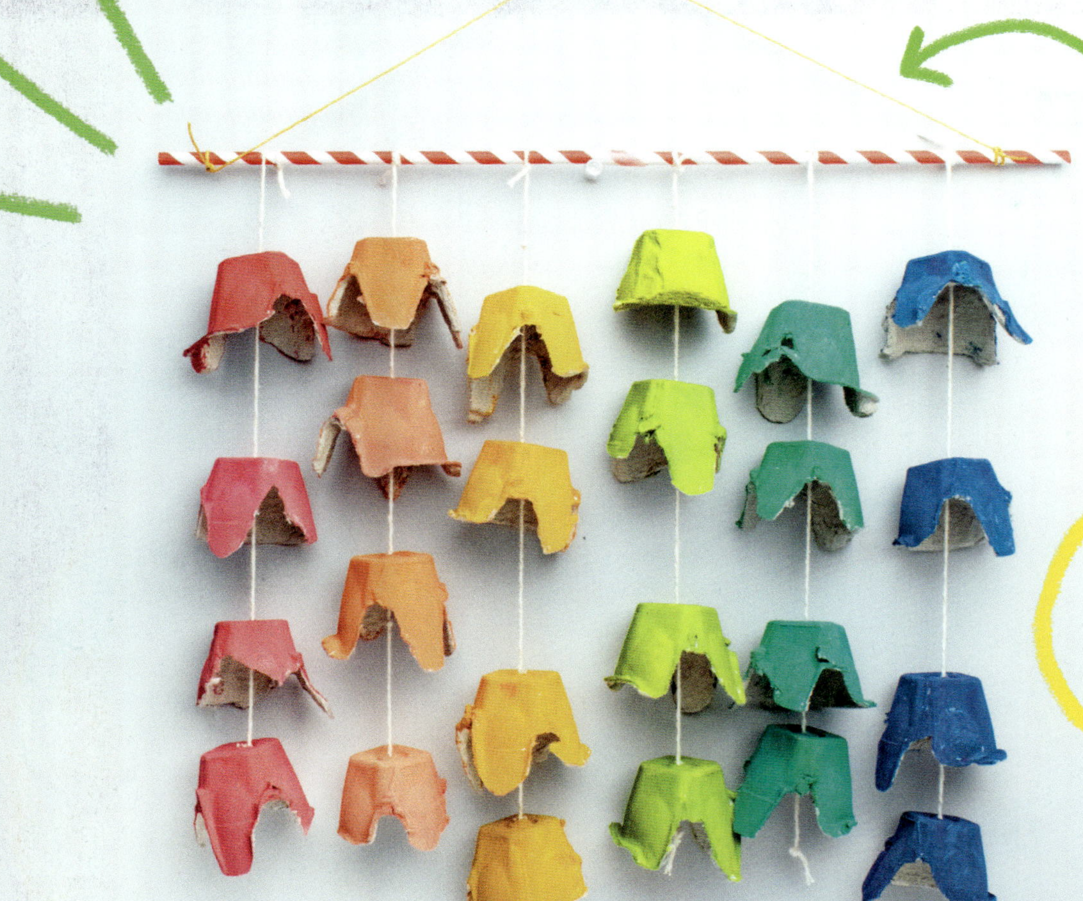

Use string and straws to hang your creation.

## Get Inspired

Look at the basic shapes of your three main materials. How can you use these shapes to inspire your creation?

## Your Turn!

What kinds of figures could you create out of egg carton cups?

What could you create using many different colors of string?

Could straws be used to make a frame?

# WEAR IT

What wearable clothing or accessories could you make from egg cartons, string, and straws?

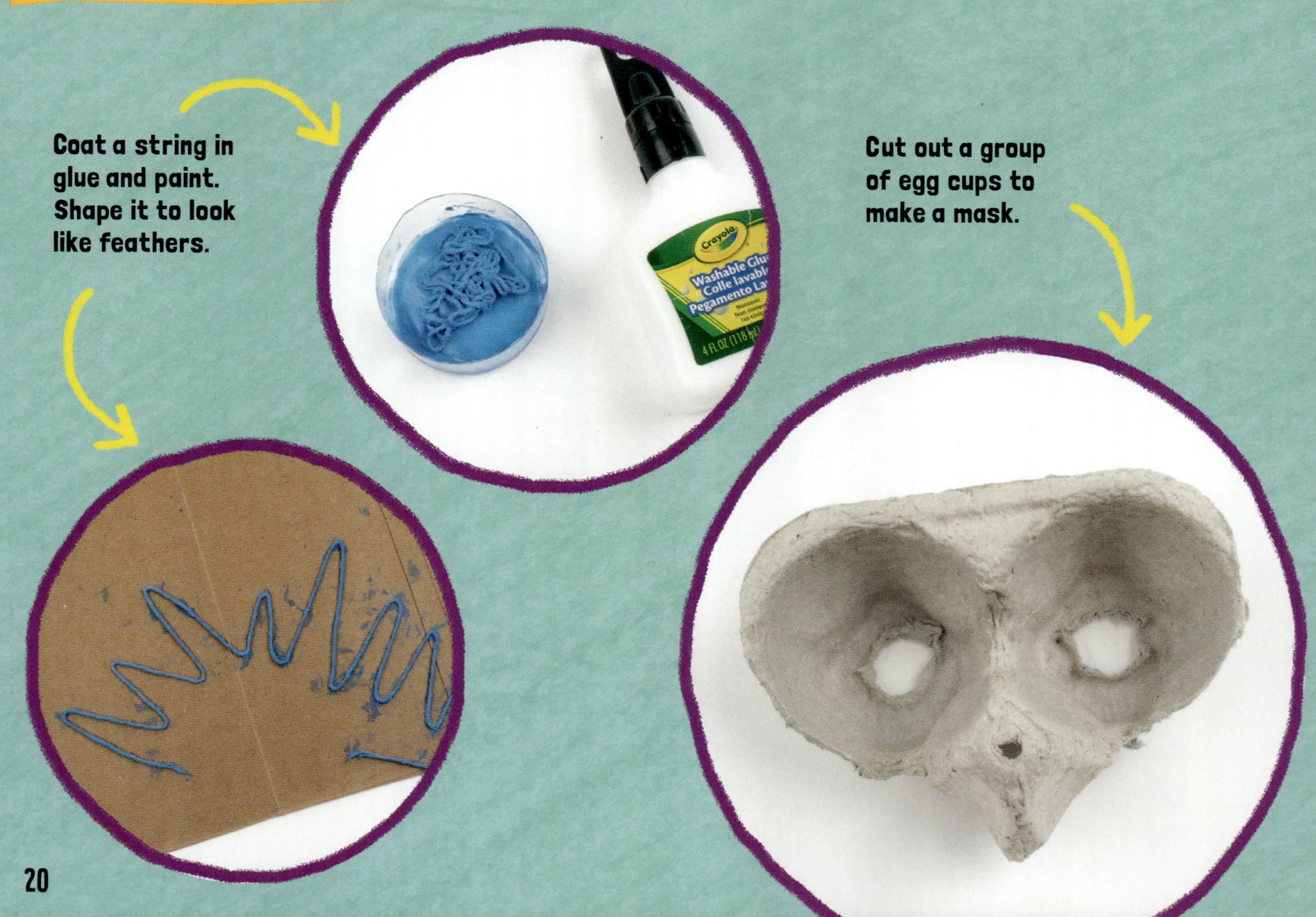


**Coat a string in glue and paint. Shape it to look like feathers.**

**Cut out a group of egg cups to make a mask.**

## Problem-Solve

Every problem has a solution. Are you tired of holding up your mask? Use string to tie it around your head!

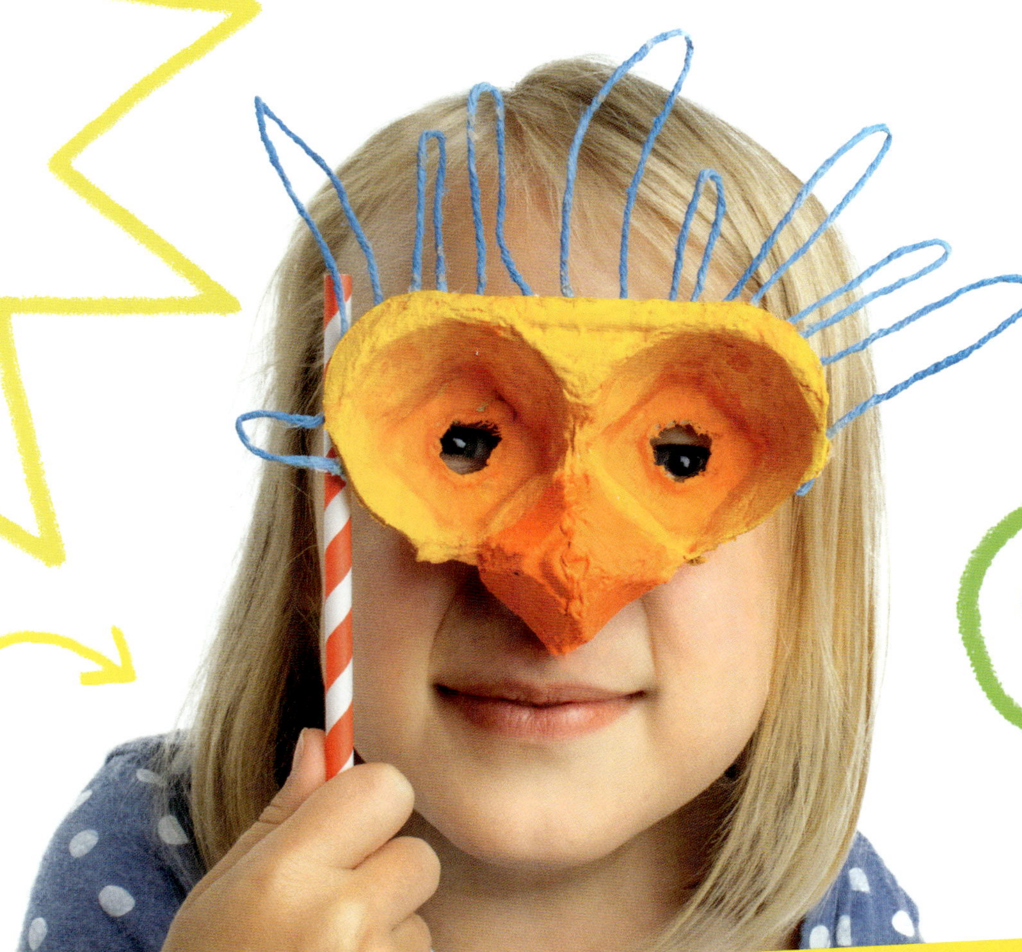

**Use a straw to hold the mask in front of your face.**

## Your Turn!

How would you turn egg carton cups into earrings?

Could you braid or knot together strings to create a bag?

Could you cut straws into small pieces to make beads?

# USE IT

Think of an item you need. Then **design** it! Egg cartons, string, and straws provide many options for functional projects.

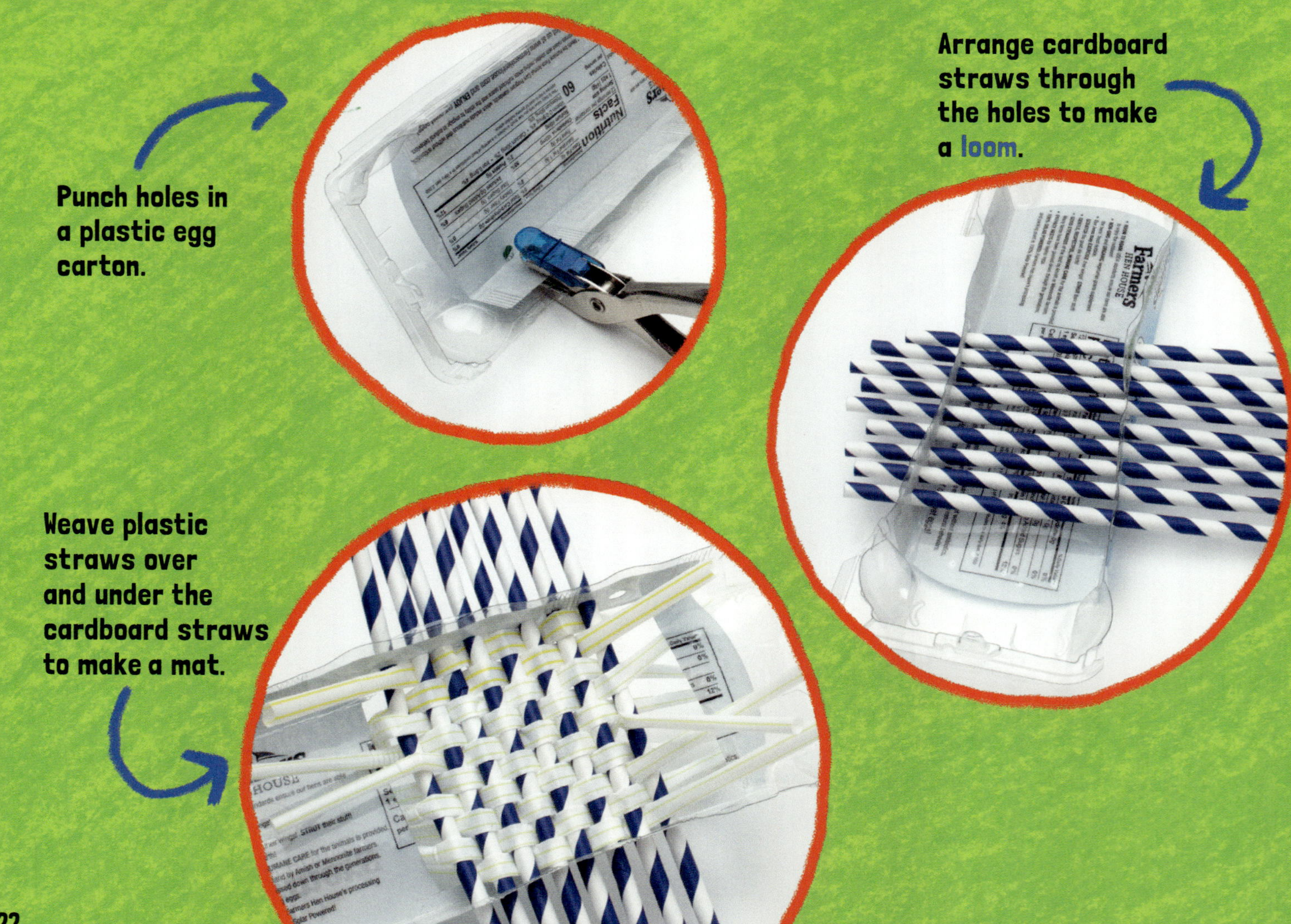

**Punch holes in a plastic egg carton.**

**Arrange cardboard straws through the holes to make a loom.**

**Weave plastic straws over and under the cardboard straws to make a mat.**

## Imagine

Imagine you needed to create an object to be used underwater. How would you need to adapt your item?

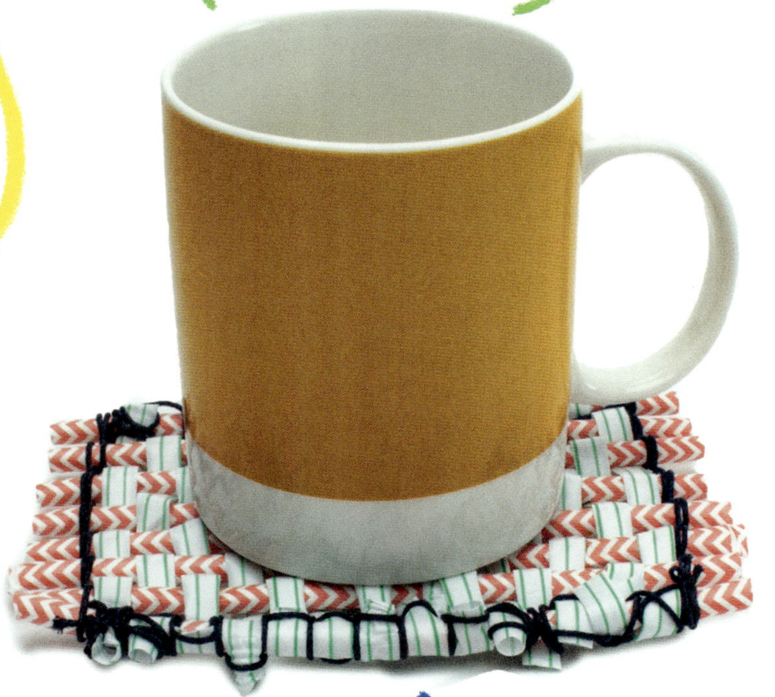

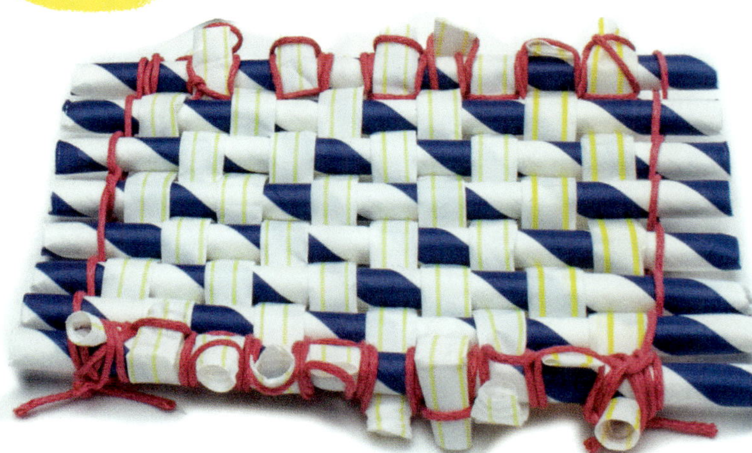

Use string to secure the edges.

Use your mat as a coaster!

## Your Turn!

Could you use egg cartons to store beads, gems, or other materials?

Can you use string to hang your item or make a pulley system for it?

Could straws be turned into handles or wheel spokes?

# BUILD IT

Engineers use all kinds of materials to build. What do you want to construct? Can you do it using only egg cartons, string, and straws?

Build a wiggly caterpillar! Thread string through egg cups. Tie knots in the string so the cups stay in place.

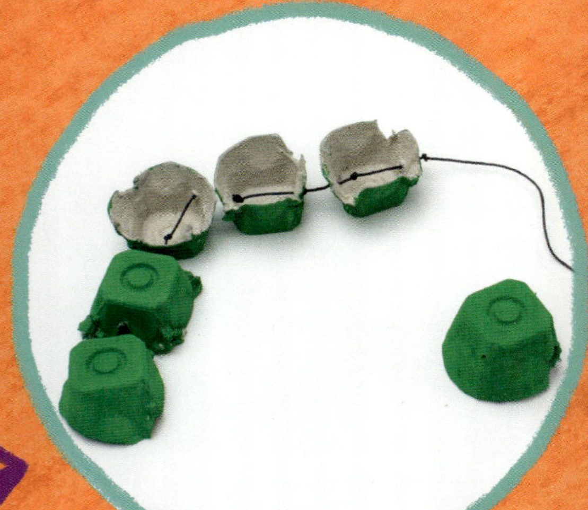

Tie knots in a bit of string. Thread the ends through a straw piece to make an antenna.

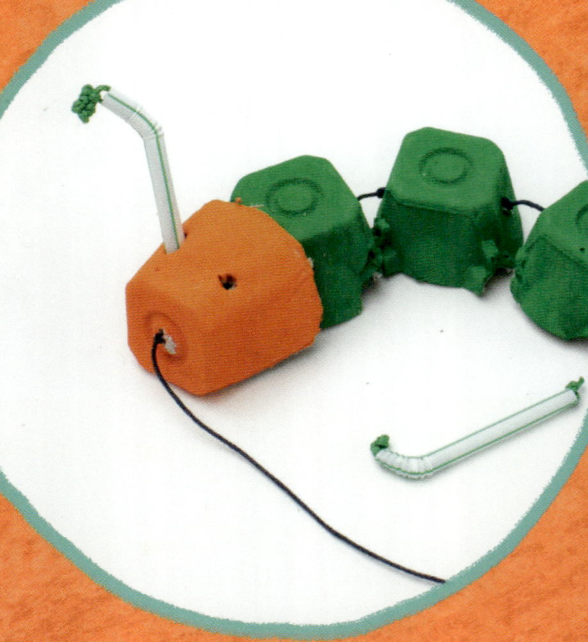

Use small pieces of string to make stripes.

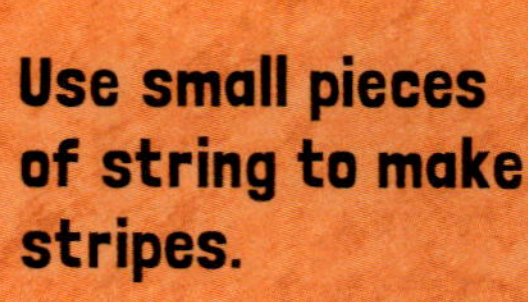

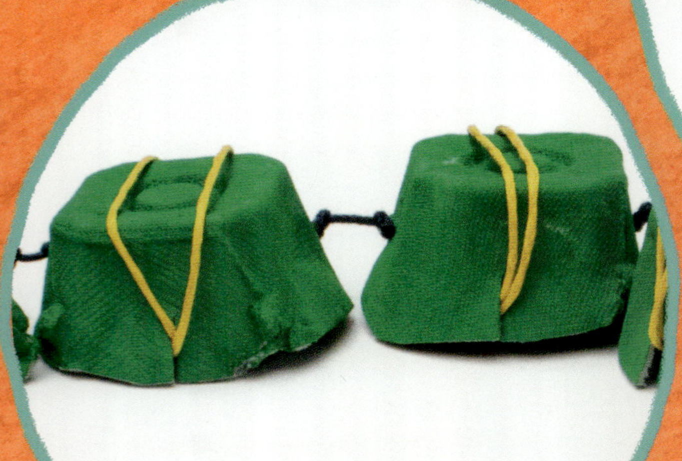

## Collaborate

Don't be afraid to ask a friend or classmate for help with your project. Other makers might have ideas you didn't think of! They can also lend a hand during construction.

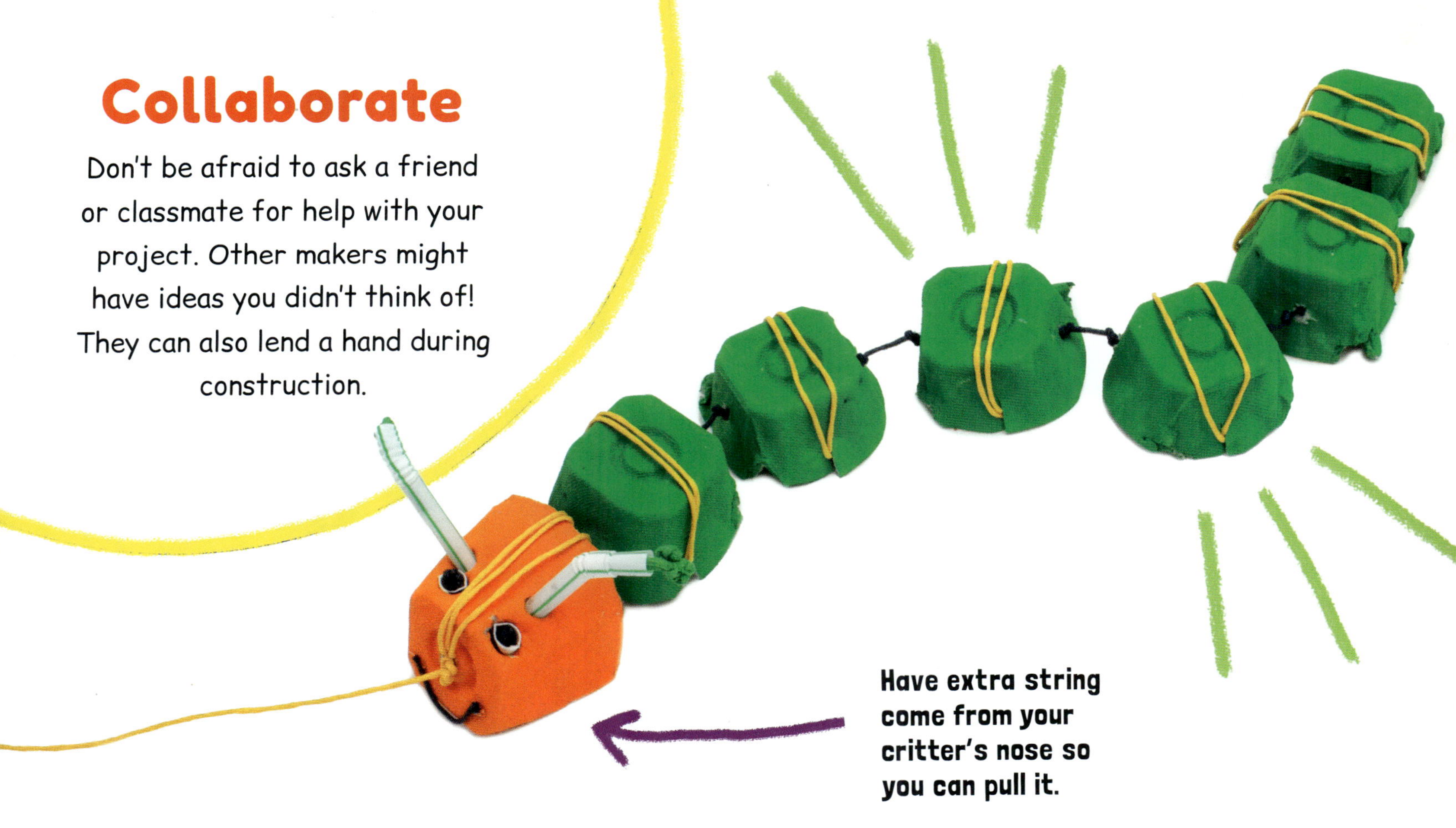

**Have extra string come from your critter's nose so you can pull it.**

## Your Turn!

Could you turn egg carton cups into train cars?

How would string be helpful in building a bridge?

How would you make a **windmill** out of straws?

# GIFT IT

Is a holiday or birthday coming up? Do you want to surprise a friend or family member just for fun? You can make all kinds of homemade gifts using egg cartons, string, and straws.

Connect egg cups in different ways to make new shapes.

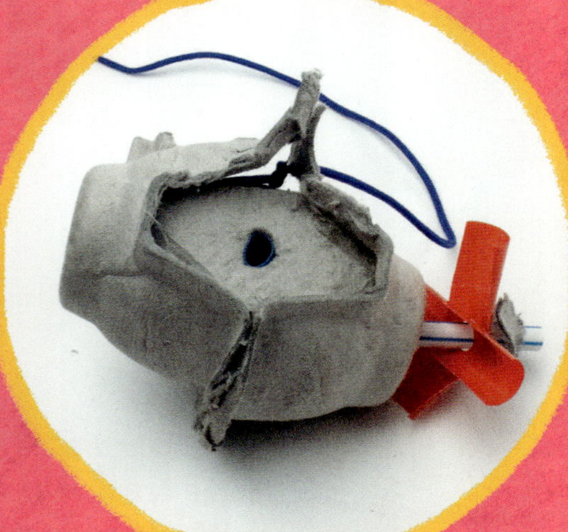

Use straw pieces to make a **propeller**.

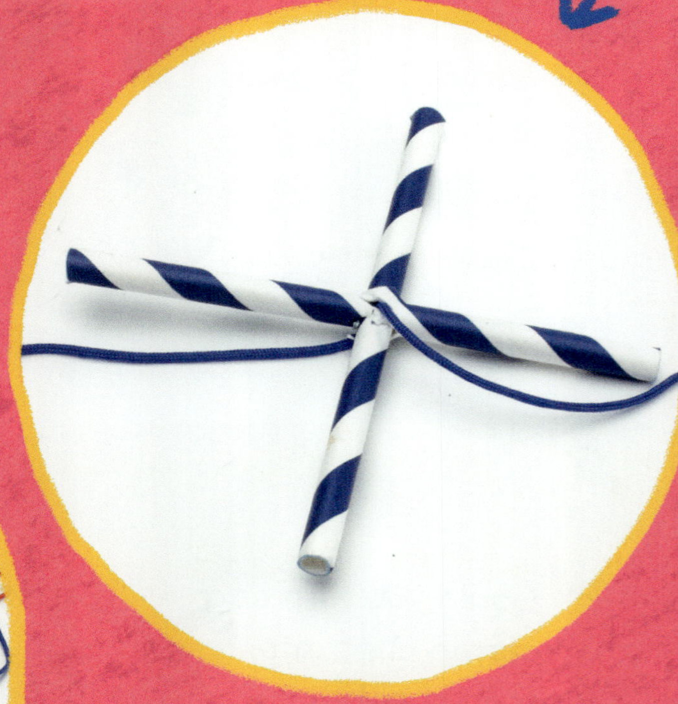

Use plastic egg cups and string to make windows.

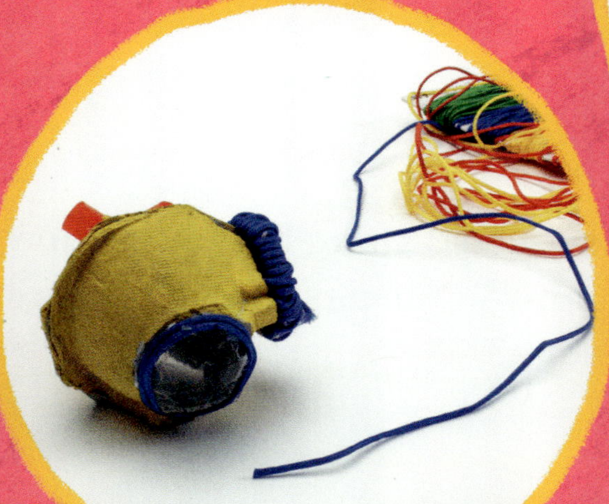

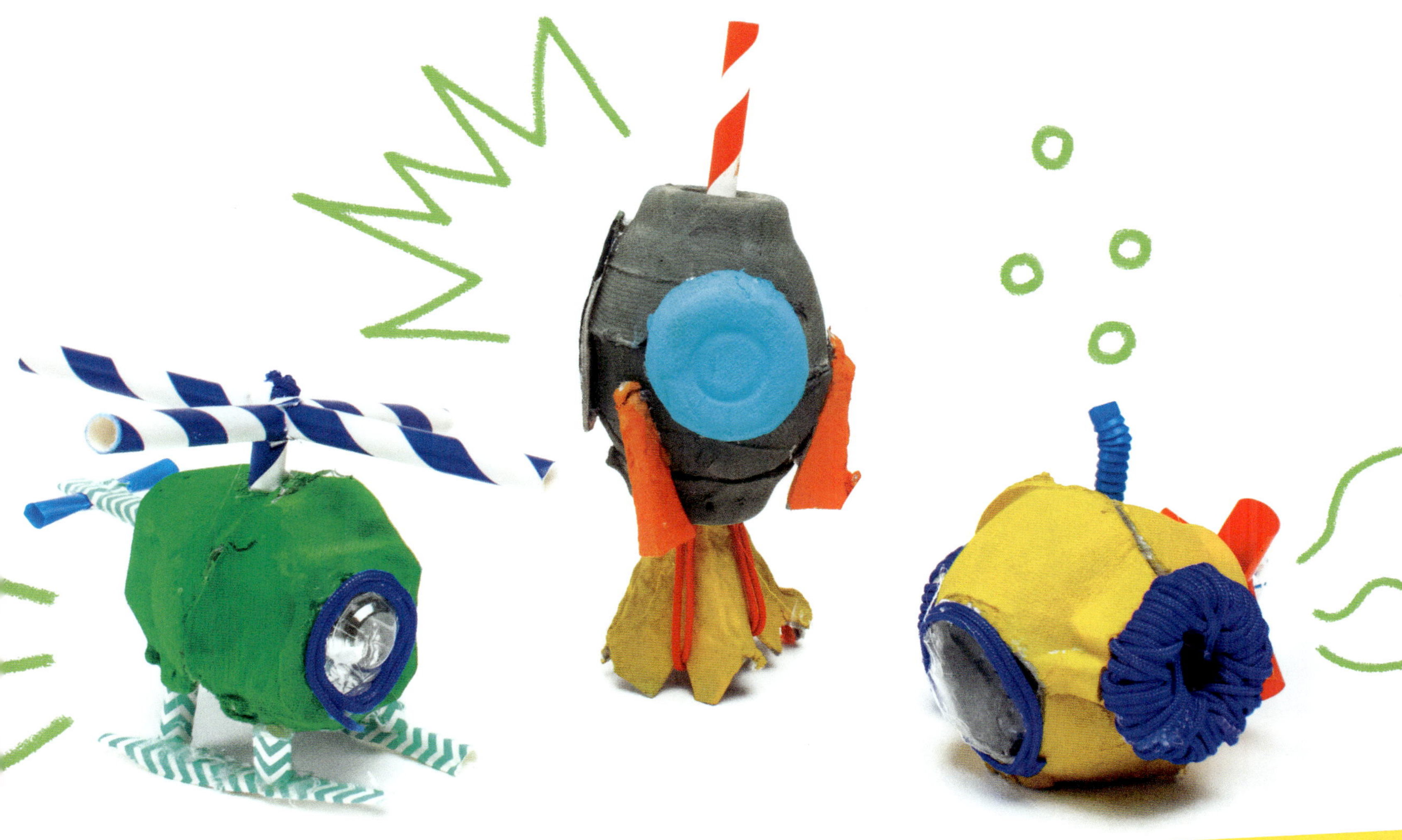

## Your Turn!

Could you turn a paper egg carton into a pop-up card?

Could you roll up balls of string to create mini animal figures?

How would you use straws to make a holiday-themed ornament?

# PLAY WITH IT

Looking for something fun to do? Use egg cartons, string, and straws to create your own toys and games!

**Glue strings inside egg cups to make tentacles.**

**Poke a hole through the center of a straw. Thread another straw through the hole to make a *T* shape.**

**Thread string through a straw to make puppet strings.**

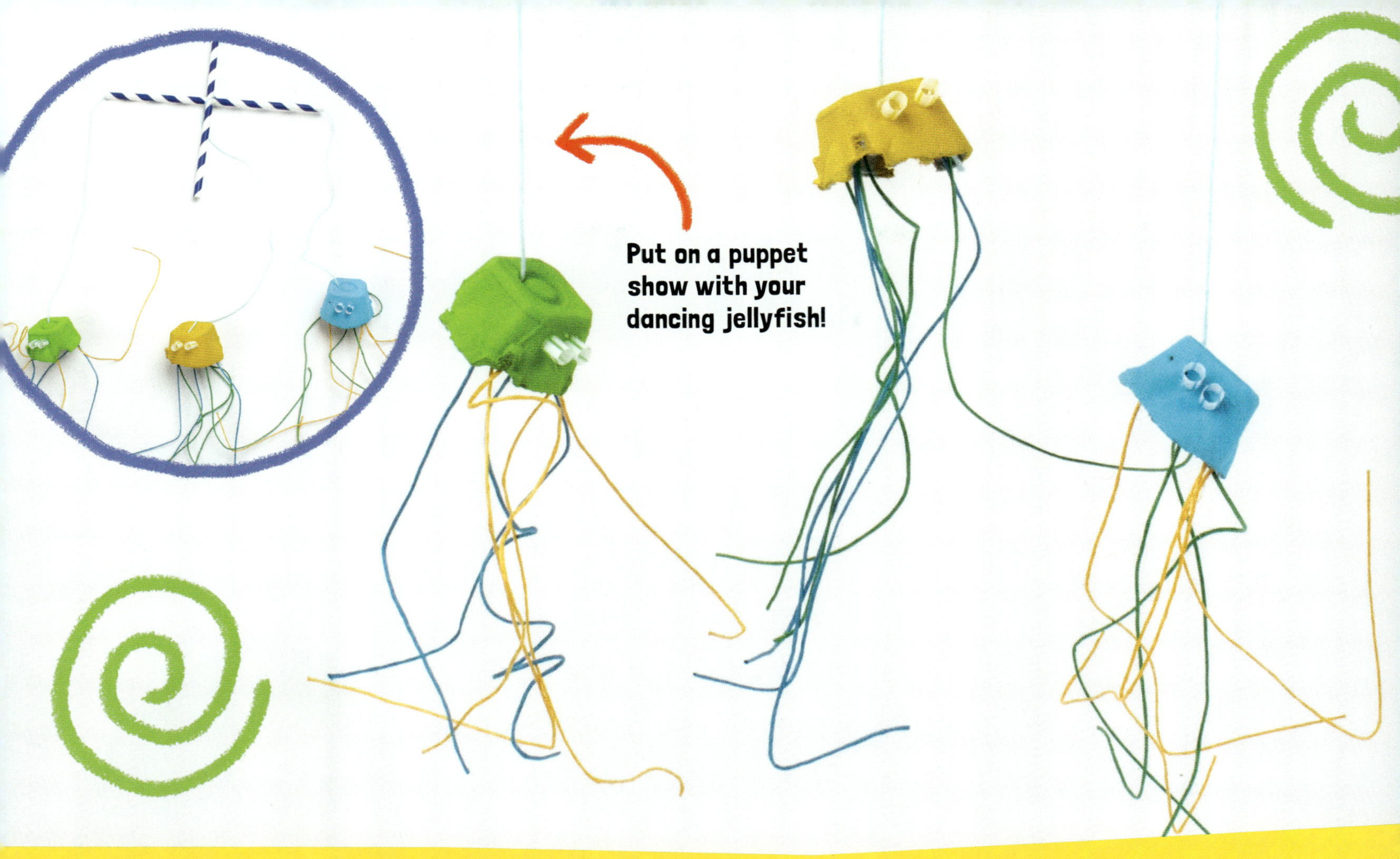


## Your Turn!

How could you turn an egg carton into a game board?

Could you make small dolls out of bundles of string?

How could you combine straws into a floating water toy?

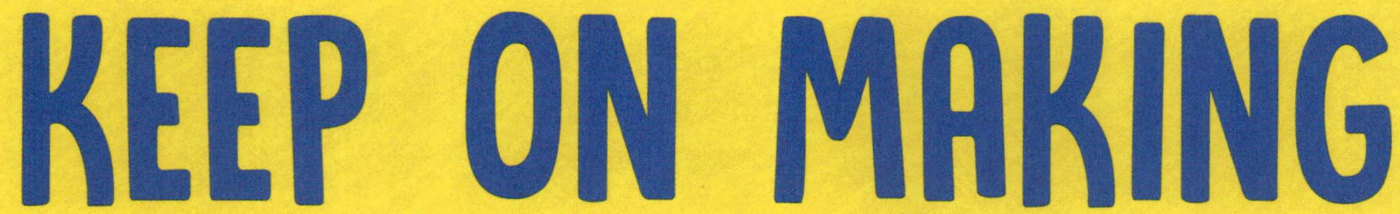

# KEEP ON MAKING

Your egg carton, string, and straw projects may look complete, but don't close your makerspace toolbox yet. Think about what would make these projects even better. What would you do differently if you made each one again? What would happen if you used different methods or added another material?

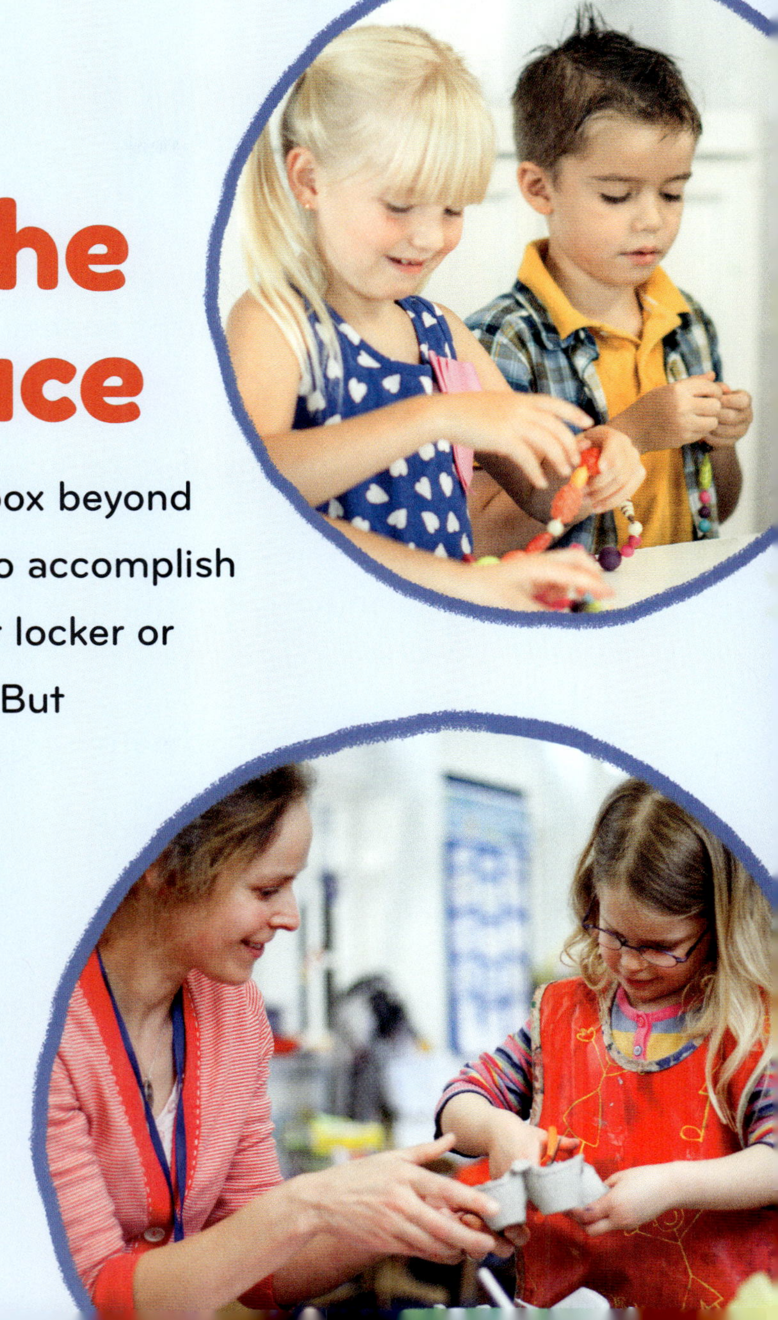

# Beyond the Makerspace

You can use your makerspace toolbox beyond the makerspace! You might use it to accomplish everyday tasks, like decorating your locker or making a birthday gift for a friend. But makers use the same toolbox to do big things. One day, these tools could help **design** homes or build supersmart robots. Turn your world into a makerspace! What problems could you solve?

# GLOSSARY

**accessory** – a piece of jewelry or clothing that makes an outfit appear more complete.

**collaboration** – the act of working with others.

**design** – to plan how something will appear or work.

**detail** – a small part of something.

**flexible** – easy to move or bend.

**loom** – a tool used for weaving.

**propeller** – a device with turning blades used to move a vehicle such as an airplane or a boat.

**pulley** – a wheel over which a rope or cable may be pulled.

**soak** – to leave something in a liquid for a while.

**solution** – an answer to, or a way to solve, a problem.

**spoke** – one of the metal rods that go from the center of a wheel to the rim.

**tentacle** – a long, flexible limb on an invertebrate such as a jellyfish or squid.

**windmill** – a structure with long blades that are pushed by the wind to produce power.